The Journey

FAITHING YOUR WAY THROUGH

CECILIA N. HUBBARD

Published by So It Is Written, LLC
Detroit, MI
SoItIsWritten.net

The Journey: Faithing Your Way Through

Edited by: So It Is Written – www.SoItIsWritten.net

Formatting: Ya Ya Ya Creative – YaYaYaCreative@gmail.com

ISBN: 979-8-9912588-0-7

LCCN: 2024915959

PRINTED AND BOUND IN THE UNITED STATES OF AMERICA

TABLE OF CONTENTS

INTRODUCTION

I'm not sure if we, as believers of God, truly embody faith the way that we should. When I think about the life of faith as the chosen people of God, we often find ourselves caught up in routines and rituals. Sometimes, we forget the deeper essence of what it means to live a life of faith. True faith isn't about how often we attend a Sunday morning service. It's not about how well you can quote Scripture. It's not even about how eloquent your prayers are. It's about embodying the essence of faith and literally being bold enough to carry the call to trust in the unseen. It's the mandate to hold onto hope even in the darkest times.

Faith challenges us to see beyond our immediate circumstances. It challenges us to believe in the higher purpose and plan of God. As believers, we must continuously reflect on our actions and intentions, ensuring that they align with the values we profess. In essence, living a life of faith is a journey of constant growth and self-improvement. It invites us to be better versions of ourselves, to forgive and seek forgiveness, and to remain steadfast in our convictions. It's about finding strength in our beliefs and allowing that strength to guide us through life's many trials and triumphs.

As we journey through life, we navigate the complexities and uncertainties as they come our way. This book is a companion for those who seek to deepen their understanding and relationship with God. It offers insights and reflections on the profound impact faith can have on our daily lives. Faith in God is not just a passive belief; it's an active one. It's a dynamic force that guides us, comforts us, and provides us with hope and resilience.

Faith in God serves as an anchor that holds us steady in the vicissitudes of life. It's the light that illuminates our path when the way forward seems gripped with fog. Through short descriptions, Scriptural references, and practical advice, this book aims to inspire and strengthen your faith, helping you to see God's hand at work in every aspect of your journey.

Faith is not a destination. It's a continuous journey marked by both challenges and triumphs. As we delve deeper into our spiritual lives, we uncover the layers of our beliefs and the strength that lies within them. This book is crafted to be your guide and companion, offering solace during moments of doubt and celebrating with you in times of joy. In the upcoming pages, we will delve into the transformative power of prayer, the importance of community in fostering faith, and the significance of gratitude in our daily ives.

This journey will serve as a testament to the resilience of the human spirit and the boundless possibilities that faith can unlock. We will also address common issues and doubts that often arise on this spiritual path. It is natural to question and seek understanding, and this book encourages an open and honest exploration of those feelings. By confronting our uncertainties, we can build a more profound, authentic connection with our faith. Throughout this journey, remember that faith is a deeply personal experience. While the path may be unique for each of us. the underlying principles of love, trust and hope remain universal.

As you read, reflect on your own experiences, and allow the insights shared here to resonate with your heart. May this book be a beacon of light, guiding you through the complexities of life and helping you to discover the divine presence in every moment. Together, we will embrace the beauty of faith, nurture our spiritual growth, and find peace in the knowledge that we are held by a love greater than we can imagine.

I also want this to serve as a realistic record while our faith is anchored in God as our pillar, our foundation, and our strong tower. What happens when it seems as if we are no longer attached? What happens to our solid foundation? Where is your faith now? Maybe those questions are not for you. Maybe you have always been locked in and secure in your faith. Personally, that's not my testimony. I recall when the faith that I *said* I had resembled the total *opposite*. Have you ever been there? Every step felt like walking through a dense fog during a period of doubt and uncertainty. I questioned my beliefs, my purpose, and my path. Yet, in those moments of confusion, I found the strength to seek answers and embrace the journey of self-discovery. Through prayer and reflection, I began to rebuild my faith piece by piece. I became a building block for a stronger, more resilient spirit. I learned that faith isn't about having all the answers; it's about trusting the process and believing in the beauty of growth in the one who does.

The journey hasn't always been this way. There was a time when I didn't experience this grand faith. I heard people speak of it. However, I felt that the error in my ways was nonexistent in conjunction with the trials and tribulations of life. I found myself questioning this whole life of faith. Many questions flooded my mind. I felt as if God didn't care about me. It was as if I'd lost communication with Him. The more I knocked, the more it felt as if I was standing on the edge of an abyss. I found myself staring into the vast emptiness. What seemed to be unanswered prayers echoed back, amplifying my sense of isolation. Yet, amidst the turmoil, a spark of hope refused to be extinguished. Even when I found myself repeatedly asking God, *"Why? Why are bad things happening to me? What did I do wrong?"* I was caught up in who I was as a person and believer in Christ. After my questions, Holy Spirit whispered to me, urging me to persevere, and to seek understanding and solace in the midst of daunting experiences.

One day, I was worried about a situation. I had to make a decision and make it fast. As I drove, I heard Holy Spirit ask, *"Will you trust me? What do you see?"* From that encounter, I knew the faith I said I had vs. the faith I was operating in were not one in the same. I understood the pressure that was being applied to this "faith," which was the size of a mustard seed. This revelation and divine impartation produced the belief, hope, and trust required for any test. From there, the Holy Spirit led me to Hebrews 11:1:

> *"Now faith is the substance of things hoped for, the evidence of things not seen."*

I don't know about you, but when I *think* of all the Lord has done to my soul, my heart leaps with much gratitude and compassion. He didn't have to, but He did what He did anyhow! Because he loves me, he cares for me. I am His own! Hallelujah! There is no greater relationship than the one we have with God—the Creator, the author and the finisher of our faith. It is essential that we take hold of God's promises over our lives—not just take hold of the promises—but intentionally declare them until we see the manifestation of His glory. It's amazing how so many people value man's words, but question God's words (promises) on every turn. Man will fail us; however, God will *never* fail us.

Remember-GOD is not a man, so he does not lie.
He is not human he does not change his mind.
Has he ever spoken and failed to act?
Has he ever promised and not carried it through?
-NUMBERS 23:19 (NLT)

So, I pray today that if you find yourself lacking the assurance of the faith in God, it's time to recalibrate. Choose to get into an intimate relationship with God. Today can be a fresh start if you want it. You must have a willing and seeking heart. Start with conversation with God. Pray and ask for the direction of the Holy Spirit and speak God's Word over your life. Get the Word of Truth, read it, and believe it. Declare and activate the words that the Lord has already commanded you to do by faith daily. Speak the Word loudly and boldly. Command His promises—not just over your own life—but over the lives of your family, your children, and your brothers and sisters in Christ.

Stand firm. Stand or faith with trust, belief and hope. The way has already been made. All God had to do was speak the words in Genesis, "Let there be," and it was! So, I pray that you would do the same: Speak with power and authority and believe that it will be according to God's will.

As you cascade your way through, faithing your way through this journey, grab hold of your faith, be vigilant, be thankful, and stay prayerful. Allow the manifestation of God's glory and the guidance of the Holy Spirit to do what only He can do. Now, it's time. Faithing your way through the journey has begun. Remember:

Without faith, it is impossible to please God.
-HEBREWS 11:6 (NIV)

WHAT IS FAITH?

*B*efore we discuss what faith is, according to biblical truth, let's dispel what faith is *not*.

- † Faith is *not* a feeling.

- † Faith is *not* an event.

- † Faith is *not* an intellectual stance.

- † Faith is *not* the premise or preference of man.

- † Faith is *not* positive thinking.

- † Faith is *not* shouting and praying for something hard enough until it appears.

Now that we've got all of the mirages of faith out of the way, let's dissect what the Bible says about faith. The Greek mythology Pistis the personification of good *faith* in the New Testament. *Pistis* is translated as faith. We already laid out what faith is *not*. Faith is your belief led by your action. *Faith* is an active trust in God!

*"Now faith is the assurance of things hoped for,
the conviction of things not seen."*
-HEBREWS 11:1 (ESV)

This Scripture is the biblical definition of what *faith* actually is. There are many scriptural references that provide illustrations of faith in the Bible. For the sake of defining faith, we will journey through a few.

James 2:26 (ESV) says, *"For as the body apart from the spirit is dead, so also faith apart from works is dead."* In this text, James merely demonstrates his faith through his own works. Let's be honest: The action shows what we believe by what we engage in or what we choose *not* to engage in. Some may have heard the example of faith concerning a chair. I "believe" that the chair has the capacity to hold me; however, my action by sitting down represents the faith I've placed in the chair. Have you ever questioned God's capacity, but trusted the chair blindly? It's a curious contradiction. We often place unwavering faith in everyday objects, like a chair, without a second thought. Yet, our minds are filled with doubt and questions when it comes to larger, more profound concepts, such as the divine. This paradox highlights the complexity of human belief and the nature of trust.

Hebrews 11:6 (NIV) says, *"And without faith, it is impossible to please God because anyone who comes to* him must believe that he exists and that he rewards those who earnestly seek him." If we do not trust that God is in fact real, and that what He says is accurate, we won't be saved. You may ask, "How can you make a statement like that?" It is recorded in Ephesians 2:8-10 (NIV): "For it is by grace you have been saved, through faith—and this is not from yourselves, it is the gift of God— not by works, so that no one can boast. For we are God's handiwork, created in Christ Jesus to do good works, which God prepared in advance for us to do."

We were born as sinners who deserve the ultimate punishment. However, because we believe in Jesus, because we believe He has come to save the world and that He come to die on our behalf, and He was raised with all power. It is yet our trust that Jesus saved us from our sins, and He gives the Holy Spirit, as He promised. The promise recorded in John 14:15-17 (NIV) says, "If you love me, keep my commands. And I will ask the Father, and he will give you another advocate to help you and be with you forever— the Spirit of truth. The world cannot accept him because it neither sees him nor knows him. But you know him, for he lives with you and will be in you." Second Corinthians 5:17 (NKJV) says, "Therefore, if anyone is in Christ, he is a new creation; old things have passed away; behold, all things have become new." Now, that's faith.

If your faith doesn't emulate what the Scripture says, today you have the opportunity to make the change. From this day forward, may the life you live as a believer rest upon the purpose and foundation of God. If you are wondering how to increase your faith, follow the words written in Romans 10:17.

> *"So then faith cometh by hearing,*
> *and hearing by the word of God."*
> ROMANS 10:17 (KJV)

The point is: *Before you trust, you have to listen. But unless Christ's Word is preached, there's nothing to listen to.*

As you journey through this transformative power of faith and the importance of embracing it in every aspect of life, I hope to inspire you to listen deeply, trust wholeheartedly, and "faith" your way through challenges and triumphs alike. By anchoring yourself in the teachings of Christ and opening your heart to His Word, you can navigate the complexities of life with grace, confidence, and unwavering hope. May this journey enrich your perspective, enlighten your soul, and strengthen your spirit—cultivating a guiding light as you cascade through a life filled with purpose and a deeper connection to the divine.

FAITH OVER FEAR

For God has not given us a spirit of fear and timidity,
but of power, love, and self-discipline.
2 TIMOTHY 1:7 (NLT)

Fear is a simple word; yet, it can carry significant volume. It is a word that many know far too well; yet, many are afraid to confront it. If one is not careful, fear can cause a great deal of destruction. Unfortunately, fear has placed an entrenched imprint on the lives of many, causing it to speak louder than faith. Fear has robbed many and caused some to devalue their ability to produce beyond what their eyes can see.

The enemy is the creator of fear. His job is to steal joy, kill peace, ruin your purpose, and demolish your most valuable jewel—your relationship with God. All the while, the enemy is depositing stress and insecurities. If you'll be honest, it will cause you to doubt God and His abilities. God knew long before your creation that you would be subject to fear. These commands, "Don't fear" and "Do not doubt" are written in the Bible more than three hundred times, which suggests that God already knew what we would be up against. No longer will we entertain the lies and schemes of the enemy. Even when Satan begins to whisper things like, "You can't recover from the divorce," or "You will never get over your past," rebuke it! Speak back to that voice using the Word of God.

God is in control of all things. The only responsibility we have in what may seem to be an unfavorable situation is to grab hold of our faith—our trust in God and stand on His Word. His Word will not return to you void. It is time to stand as warriors, taking a new approach to the word "F.E.A.R." (Facing Everything and Responding). Today, I declare an increase of faith and a release of the chains. Walk boldly with your head held high. You are set free!

Father, I pray that every day you allow our eyes to open, there will be an increase in my faith, trust, and assurance in you. Even in the moments when the enemy tries to infiltrate my mind with fear, God, give the courage and wisdom to stand on your Word.

In Jesus' Name. Amen.

1. Have you identified your fear?

_____

_____

_____

_____

_____

2. How has it affected your forward movement?

_____

_____

_____

_____

_____

3. What actions will you take to break free from the chains?

_____

_____

_____

_____

_____

YOU ARE A WINNER

Don't you realize that in a race everyone runs,
but only one person gets the prize? So run to win!
-1 CORINTHIANS 9:24 (NLT)

efore you were born, God predestined you. Before your mother had a notion of your existence, purpose was already established. The journey that has been set explicitly for you is covered in power, enriched by an anointing that only you can fulfill. It is attached with a godly boldness, linked to a lane with your name engraved in it. While cascading through the channels of life, circumstances that flow from it sometimes have the potential to make you feel like the opposite of a winner. Life has been filled with daunting experiences and discouraging moments. Sometimes, you may feel unsure and unqualified for your assignment. Keep this in mind: The Lord told the prophet Jeremiah, *"Before I formed you in your mother's womb, I knew you"* and *"Before you were born, I set you apart."* Just as those words were spoken to Jeremiah, they also apply to you. There is a divine purpose and call on your life that only you can fulfill. As you run your race, I pray that, with each stride, your head is held high while carrying the confidence and godly boldness that is deep down inside of you. Keep going and don't look back. Even in the stumbles, God is always nearby. Keep going; you're almost there! Remember: You are a winner!

Lord, as I run this race, I pray that you will give confidence, strength, and endurance until the end. At the moment of uncertainty, please provide a gentle reminder of the torch that you have given me to carry.

In Jesus' name. Amen.

Meditation Moments

1. Do you believe what God has said about you?

   _____

   _____

   _____

   _____

   _____

2. Do you know what your purpose is? If not, have you prayed and asked God about it?

   _____

   _____

   _____

   _____

   _____

3. In what area(s) of your life have you been stagnant?

    _____

    _____

    _____

    _____

    _____

4. How will you navigate through these area(s)?

    _____

    _____

    _____

    _____

    _____

OBEDIENCE IS KEY

The Lord had said to Abram,
"Go from your country, your people and
your father's household to the land I will show you."
−GENESIS 12:1 (NIV)

There are many things that come with *next*. The uncertainty of the next step can be frightening. It can potentially cause hesitation as you attempt to move beyond the familiar place. Moving in a direction where you can't fully see, and not knowing what lies ahead, can be scary.

As you allow faith to dwell in those unsure places, and commit to follow God's instruction, the reward is revealed. It is imperative that the moment God speaks, your response immediately follows His words without delay. Your response should be a simple, "Yes," while being devoted and intentional to carrying out your assignment by following His directives. There is no time to question God. At the moment God told Abraham to go, not once did Abraham complain, compare or question God. Abraham operated in faithfulness, and he operated in obedience the first time God gave the instruction. Just imagine if we operated as such, allowing our obedience to be the first movement.

In the following few verses of Genesis 12, it is revealed that there was a reward waiting for him. However, what was so remarkable in the passage is that the first thing shown on the instruction was not what he would gain. The Bible declares in Psalm 37:23, *The steps of a good man are ordered by the LORD: And he delighteth in his way. Though he fall, he shall not be utterly cast down: For the LORD upholdeth him with his hand.* Whose direction will you follow? Your own path or God's?

Father, allow me to listen to your voice, words, and instruction without question or delay. I surrender to your will, O'Lord. I put my agenda aside. Holy Spirit, guide me without hesitation or delay.

In Jesus' name. Amen.

Meditation Moments

1. Whose direction are you following?

   _____

   _____

   _____

   _____

   _____

2. Do you obey God's directives the *first* time?

   _____

   _____

   _____

   _____

   _____

3. What areas do you need help with regarding your
    obedience?

    _____

    _____

    _____

    _____

    _____

ONE STEP AT A TIME

For we live by faith, not by sight.
–2 CORINTHIANS 5:7 (NIV)

If God provided every detail, would we need faith? Probably not. How can we say we have faith if we never experience what it takes to gain it? Granted, faith is a gift, and everyone was dealt a measure of it. As with anything else, it is our responsibility to exercise faith and not become complacent or lazy with it. Like a muscle, in order for it to grow, it must be strengthened by weightlifting. Faith is not something that magically appears or something that we just stumble upon. Faith is something that must be built.

Life has a way of testing you. Life will cause you to put your faith in motion through reading the Word, communicating with God by way of prayer, and establishing an authentic relationship with Him. When we operate in faith, we totally trust, rely, and depend on

God, no matter what. It's not the easiest thing to do; however, it is necessary. The more you find yourself imploring God, getting into His presence, having more conversations, applying the principle of the Word of truth, the more your faith will be ignited. Watch what God will do if you step out on faith.

Declare these words:

HIS WILL+HIS WAY= MY FAITH

Father,
Today, I choose to walk by faith and
not by what I see in the natural.
I choose to rest in your will,
even though I don't fully know or understand.
I choose to heed to your voice only.

In Jesus' name. Amen.

 *Meditation Moments*

1. Are you ready to relinquish control and submit to/trust God?

_____

_____

_____

_____

_____

2. In what area(s) do you find your faith lacking?

_____

_____

_____

_____

_____

3. In what ways have you started to build your faith?

_____

_____

_____

_____

_____

Gentle reminder:

Faith, the size of a mustard seed,
can move mountains.
-MATTHEW 17:20 (NIV)

THE JOURNEY
RELINQUISH CONTROL

---

*Trust in the LORD with all your heart and lean not on
your own understanding; in all your ways submit to
him, and he will make your paths straight.*
−PROVERBS 3:5-6 (NIV)

---

*L*ife is as much about the journey and the experience as it is about the destination. Let's avoid getting entangled by our own agenda; slow down and pay attention. You have probably missed so many things because of the urgency of the demand and expectations you have placed on moments. You have mentally and physically extended yourself during times when you were supposed to be still. You've overanalyzed situations. In those moments, all you were supposed to do was *trust God*. You've been seeking answers, and there are things that God has been trying to release and reveal along the path. However, because of your interjection, you've produced the preconceived notion that it is now or never. In some cases, urgency is necessary. Through your journey, some unfavorable circumstances have left you feeling broken, bitter, and confused. In some instances, God has been trying to grow your faith. There have been exit signs you have passed, and there have been entrances you did not walk through.

In some cases, you didn't see them because you were moving too fast. If you're honest, there were some things you ignored (i.e., the warning signs) and yielded on your trail because you did not fully trust God. But today, you have another chance to start over. Release yourself, your timeline, and your agenda. You can no longer worry about tomorrow. The Word of the Lord tells us not to worry about tomorrow, for tomorrow will worry about itself; God is trying to get your attention to assure you that because He is your faith's author and finisher, your story has already been written, and the promise is waiting for you.

"The only impossible journey is the one without Christ."

Heavenly Father, I come before you today with a heart full of trust and a spirit willing to follow wherever you lead. In the journey of life, I have made a solemn declaration to trust in your ways above my own, recognizing that your wisdom far surpasses my understanding. This choice to follow you, to lay down my own paths and desires in favor of your divine plans is a testament of my faith. In Jesus' name. Amen.

Meditation Moments

1. Is your faith in God conditional?

_____

_____

_____

_____

_____

2. Do you find yourself worrying about the situation?

_____

_____

_____

_____

_____

3. Do you feel the need to always be in control?

_____

_____

_____

_____

_____

THE SECRET PLACE

*But you, when you pray, go into your room,
and when you have shut your door, pray to your
Father who is in the secret place; and your Father
who sees in secret will reward you openly.*
–MATTHEW 6:6 (NKJV)

*L*et this be the tone. Let this be an intentional connection/communication with God. Do not allow anything to prevent you from dwelling in your secret place. Intimate relationship and communion with the Father must mean more than a quick one-second prayer as you bless your food. No other conversation should ever be held to higher esteem with value and intentionality or passion as the one you desire to cultivate daily with God. With prayer and supplication, you give Holy Spirit free will to navigate your life. The Bible is our blueprint; we don't have all of the answers to this thing called life, but God does. The Scripture will guide you as you look to connect with God in a more intimate way, knowing His promises, His purpose and plan for the lives of the believers.

† In the secret place, revelation is given.

† In the secret place, strength, wholeness and unconditional love is acquired.

† In the secret place, even in the most unfavorable situations, peace is given.

† In the secret place, burdens are unveiled in exchange for liberty.

† In the secret place, one comes in broken, and exits with wholeness and assurance.

As you dwell in the secret place, set time aside to get close to the one who knows more about you than you know about yourself. Get into His presence and dwell there. Lay at His feet. It is not only tangible, but also essential, which is a divine relationship. Most importantly, go in with an open, humble heart and mind. Give thanks for who He is in your life, and tell God how you feel, while holding nothing back. Ask the Holy Spirit for guidance, allowing Him to do the rest while you're in His presence in your secret place.

Father, thank you for access to the throne of grace. Thank you for not only hearing but also answering prayers. As I seek you in this place of worship, I pray there will be divine impartation; I come seeking you, not things. I come that there would be evidence that I have spent time with you in my secret place.
In Jesus' name. Amen.

Meditation Moments

1. Do you desire a deeper, more intimate relationship with God?

   _____

   _____

   _____

   _____

   _____

2. In your prayer time, do you ask/allow the Holy Spirit to lead and guide you?

   _____

   _____

   _____

   _____

   _____

3. How do you go to God in prayer? What is your
    environment like? Are there any things that could
    cause distraction?

    _____

    _____

    _____

    _____

    _____

4. How is the posture of your heart?

    _____

    _____

    _____

    _____

    _____

CALLED BY NAME

*Moses said to the Lord, "Pardon your servant, Lord.
I have never been eloquent, neither in the past
nor since you have spoken to your servant.
I am slow of speech and tongue."*
-EXODUS 4:10 (NIV)

*H*ow many signs do you need? After the evidence has been given, you're still holding onto what you feel. Just as Moses, you tell God, your creator, to let someone else fulfill your assignment because you don't think you have what it takes.

Stop retreating, Stop disqualifying yourself with the doubt. The day has come for you to operate in your God-given call with the strength He has given and the ability He's equipped you with. In Jeremiah 29:11 (NLT), God said, For *I know the plan(s) I have for you, declares the Lord, plans to prosper, plans to give you hope and c future.* No matter what you may view as a deficiency, God views it as a masterpiece that He created, produced and cultivated. It is time for you to view yourself as such. Instead of shrinking, believe it with your whole heart.

Can you recall a time when God called you to do something, and the only thing that you could offer in return was an excuse for not fulfilling the assignment?

"God, I can't do it because I don't know how."

"God, there are so many other people who are more qualified than I am."

"God, I am too old."

"God, what will my friends and family think?"

We are all imperfect people, created by a perfect God. Rest in the fact that He has called you specifically. Get out of your emotions. Stop pondering on what you feel you can't do. It's time to develop a new mindset of *I can*, and it's time to start fresh. Renew your mind and declare these words with authority: "The I AM sent me!"

Lord, forgive me for not answering when you called. Give me the peace in who you have called and commissioned me to be. There are things in me that I view as deficiencies. Please grant me the confidence and godly boldness in these areas that I view as flaws. I realize now though my sight is not yours because what I may see that poses as imperfect, you see it is a masterpiece.

Father, help my unbelief. In Jesus' name. Amen.

Meditation Moments

1. Do we all have a calling/assignment?

_____

_____

_____

_____

_____

2. Have you identified what your calling is? If not, have you asked God what it is?

_____

_____

_____

_____

_____

3. Are you fully walking in your calling? If not, what's stopping you?

_____

_____

_____

_____

_____

ANOTHER CHANCE

He who was seated on the throne said, "I am making everything new!" Then he said, "Write this down, for these words are trustworthy and true."
–REVELATION 21:5 (NIV)

he significance of these words brought joy to my spirit. When I think of the words *trustworthy* and *true*, instantly, these words come to mind: *honorable* and *faithful*. When I think of the words accurate, authentic, and genuine, they draw me back to the essence of who God is. When I think of these words, I am reminded of the profound truth and unwavering steadfastness that define His nature. Each of these words encapsulates a facet of His divine character, offering a glimpse into the boundless love and wisdom He extends to us. To be accurate is to be precise and unerring, much like the way His guidance illuminates our path with clarity and certainty. Authenticity speaks to the sincerity and realness of His presence in our lives, a constant and unfaltering support on which we can always rely. Genuine, meanwhile, reflects the deep, unfeigned love and compassion that flows from Him, an enduring testament to His caring and nurturing spirit. In moments of doubt or uncertainty, these attributes of God serve as a beacon of hope and a reminder of the enduring truth that He embodies.

We have all experienced life's difficulties. Some situations were more alarming than others. Nonetheless, we encounter things that we would rather dismiss altogether if we could. Know that every experience will not lead to obliteration.

Every tear that fell was watering the seeds that had been planted for years. Every heartbreak, and everything viewed as a setback, was simply preparation. God has given a fresh wind, producing another chance by declaring, "Everything new!" Because of that, we can vacate that old place of bondage. Some things have paralyzed us from walking when God has given us the ability and the instructions to walk again, to live again, to be *again*. No longer will you live with limited conditions, faith, drive, and self-worth. Stand with assurance, knowing that God has graced you with *another chance because of his accurate, authentic, and genuine affection for you*.

Father, allow me to listen to your voice, words, and instruction without question or delay. I surrender to your will, O'Lord. I put my agenda aside. Holy Spirit, guide me without hesitation or delay.

In Jesus' name. Amen.

 *Meditation Moments*

1. Will you believe what He said before you see what He said?

   _____

   _____

   _____

   _____

   _____

2. What has God spoken to you?

   _____

   _____

   _____

   _____

   _____

3. You have reasonability in the *new*! What will you do
   to produce what He said?

   _____

   _____

   _____

   _____

   _____

THE DETOUR

In their hearts humans plan their course,
but the LORD establishes their steps.
–PROVERBS 16:9 (NIV)

You have the bag, key, and cell phone. The car is gassed up, and it's time to head out. Get in the car, adjust the mirror, put on your favorite music, and head to the freeway. Speed up to cruise control and get comfortable as you head to your destination. Without warning, you discover the "Road Closed" sign. Before you know it, you are highly aggravated.

Have you ever encountered a situation like this before? If you haven't, I have. Let me be the first to tell you that *every detour* has a purpose. May I submit this to you? Sometimes, the detour is deliberately produced to save you. Do you believe that God is all-knowing? He's an omnipresent God, right? Do you think He loves you?

God will do things without warning. You may find yourself traveling a longer distance sometimes; there may be a different road you must take and yet, you are unfamiliar with. Building faith in such a way produces a mindset—not just from a driving standpoint—but from a spiritual stance.

I don't have to know the way; I don't have to see. I don't have to understand. God is in control. No matter where God leads, I will follow. It *must* be the mindset. Don't get upset the next time you experience a situation that takes you in a different direction. Sometimes God will cause a detour to change things that you won't willingly change. He will keep you from places and people, sometimes to route you into the direction of your promised land. If this hasn't been your viewpoint, I hope a new perspective has been implemented.

Lord, thank you for guiding me even when I thought I had the route figured out. As I continue to move throughout this journey, I submit my will to you.

I ask that your will be done. In Jesus' name. Amen.

Meditation Moments

1. Before you grasped everything, did you stop to ask God which way to go?

_____

_____

_____

_____

_____

2. Is God's will enough?

_____

_____

_____

_____

_____

3. What did the last detour teach you?

_____

_____

_____

_____

_____

THE BATTLE IS NOT YOURS

Do not take revenge, my dear friends,
but leave room for God's wrath, for it is written:
"It is mine to avenge; I will repay," says the Lord.
–ROMANS 12:19 (NIV)

G od can handle any situation better than you can. You don't have to fight or slander their name, nor will you have to justify or correct any unlawful thing that has been conjured up against you. Words can be offensive as well as hostile in those trying times. Rest in knowing that God knows all, and He sees that every battle you are subjected to isn't for you to handle. In some moments, it can be challenging to allow God to handle it; however, find peace and silence in knowing that God's got it, and He has you covered.

The first thing you must do is *forgive them* for any wrongdoing, so you don't harbor any negative feelings. From there, allow God to take the reins and guide you.

Trust in His plan and timing, even if it doesn't align with yours. Remember that forgiveness is not just for their benefit, but it is for your healing. Let go of the anger and bitterness and allow God to work in your heart and mind. He will bring justice in His way and time. So, take heart and rest, knowing you do not have to fight this. God has already finished it for you! When God is on your side, it is automatically a fixed fight.

Father, I recognize that the battle is yours, not mine. Please help me remain steadfast in your Word when I feel the urge to interfere. I trust that you have resolved every situation, regardless of the circumstance.

In Jesus' name. Amen.

Meditation Moments

1. Have you identified the situations that consume you?

_____

_____

_____

_____

_____

2. Have you forgiven your offender, even if it's you?

_____

_____

_____

_____

_____

3. What steps will you take to move forward?

_____

_____

_____

_____

_____

FORGIVENESS CAN'T BE BASED ON CONDITIONS

Bear with each other and forgive one another
if any of you has a grievance against someone.
Forgive as the Lord forgave you.
–CO_OSSIANS 3:13 (NIV)

---

*W*hat if God operated on a condition basis? We would be in a world of turmoil! What if God treated us like we treated one another? What if He said, "I'm only going to forgive if..."? What if you never get the apology? Are you going to continue to harbor ill feelings against them? Will you continue to say things like, "I'll forgive them if..."? This very well may be your response. If it is, I pray that God's peace, release, and understanding come upon you. I pray that you fully understand that the longer you're unwilling to release whatever has been done or said, the longer the situation and the offender has control over you, your peace, your mind, and even *your walk with Christ*. If you don't get anything else, please hear these words: *Forgiveness must be for you, not for those who hurt you.*

Most importantly, if we are children of God, we're supposed to operate as such. Right?

Will you continue to walk around as if they don't exist? Will you continue with the silent treatment? Unforgiveness can cause more damage than good, producing bitterness. If this is where you find yourself, you are waiting for an apology you may never receive. What if God didn't forgive you for your transgressions? No matter what we've done, God still extends grace.

> *The Lord our God is merciful and forgiving,*
> *even though we have rebelled against him.*
> –DANIEL 9:9 (NIV)

Lord, please penetrate our hearts, allowing us to extend grace to one another as you extend to us daily. Give us the heart and mind to forgive whoever has caused pain in any form. Even if we never get the apology, we still forgive.

In Jesus' name. Amen.

 **Meditation Moments**

1. What is preventing you from forgiving?

2. Do you understand that unforgiveness causes spiritual turmoil that hinders a believer's growth? How will you move beyond the hurt?

3. What steps will you take to forgive?

_____

_____

_____

_____

_____

RELEASE

Get rid of all bitterness, rage, anger, harsh words, and slander as well as all type of evil behavior. Instead, be kind to each other, tenderhearted, forgiving one another, just as God through Christ has forgiving you.
-EPHESIANS 4:31-32 (NLT)

There are some things that have been holding you captive for far too long—things that you have not told anyone about. These things are holding you back from fulfilling the life God has for you. In turn, it has caused you to live in bondage on every hand: depression, anger, and fear. Some people you've trusted and respected have hurt you, and you still haven't forgiven them. Today take off the mask of harboring the pain only because things have grown. Harboring such pain leads to a deeper pit, which will cause you to make others pay for the pain someone else caused.

Just as with anything else, there is a process. Healing won't always happen suddenly. Many of us have heard,

"Time heals all wounds." Allow God to strip away every heartache and every disappointment. Allow Him to restore, renew, and refresh.

Father, I thank you for your love. Even through the
rough times, I know that I'm never alone.
Help me to release the negative thoughts and
negative feelings I have been harboring.
These things keep me from growing in you.
Spirit of the true and living God, fall fresh on me.

I decree and declare that I have liberty today.
The chains have been released.

In Jesus' name. Amen.

 *Meditation Moments*

1. Are you ready to take the mask off?

_____

_____

_____

_____

_____

2. Have you identified the things or people you need to release in your life?

_____

_____

_____

_____

_____

3. Will you allow the Lord to restore what was once broken (trust, heart, confidence, and/or relationships)?

_____

_____

_____

_____

_____

WHAT ARE YOU SPEAKING?

Death and life are in the power of the tongue,
And those who love it will eat its fruit.
-PROVERBS 18:21 (NKJV)

*W*ords possess an immense power that can significantly impact the world around us. It's essential to understand the influence of spoken words that shape our reality. Words have the power to inspire, uplift, hinder or harm people. Words can build or destroy, whether directed at oneself or others. Matthew 15:11 highlights that what we say is more important than what we consume. Therefore, it's crucial to reflect on the significance and influence of the words we speak every day. We must take responsibility for what we say, especially when we are upset, frustrated or disappointed. We must make a conscious effort to speak positively, even when our emotions are not in sync. Proverbs 30:32 advises us if we have been foolishly speaking to stop, even if it means you physically covering your mouth. We must choose to speak life into every moment, even in times of frustration, pain or despair. It may be challenging, but we must not allow our words to interrupt or withdraw God's blessings for our lives because of what we choose to say.

Heavenly and gracious Father, help me learn and understand the use of my tongue. Help me be more cautious of my spoken words and intentions, recognizing their profound impact on my life.

In Jesus' name. Amen.

Meditation Moments

1. What type of fruit do your words bear? (positive or negative)

_____

_____

_____

_____

_____

2. Do you sincerely desire to change your language?

_____

_____

_____

_____

_____

3. What's in your heart? (*Out of the abundance of the heart speaks*, Luke 6:45)

_____

_____

_____

_____

_____

POWER OF HIS WORDS

And God said, "Let there be light,"
and there was light.
-GENESIS 1:3 (NIV)

All it takes s one word from the Master. God spoke and created everything from seemingly nothing. As you contemplate the magnitude of a single word spoken by the Master, you are drawn into the profound essence of creation itself. From the beginning, when God spoke, His words ignited the cosmos, painting the universe with vibrant hues of light and life. Each syllable carried the weight of endless possibilities, crafting a world of wonder and beauty.

It is indeed humb ing to consider how the divine utterance of *"Let there be"* can spark the birth of miracles in our lives. Through these sacred words, healing blossoms, hearts find solace, minds discover clarity, and blessings flow abundantly. The power of creation is not a distant force. It's a living truth within our grasp, reminding us of the boundless potential that resides in the spoken word.

Embrace this profound understanding and watch as new beginnings unfurl before you. Trust in the perfect timing of the God of "let there be," whose wisdom orchestrates miracles beyond our comprehension. Let this knowledge illuminate your path, guiding you toward a future where the miraculous unfolds with each breath.

Father, I thank you for every word you have spoken concerning my life. Help me to not stand in the way or be a hindrance to what you have already established.

In Jesus' name. Amen.

Meditation Moments

1. Do you know "let there be" has already been spoken? You are just waiting for it?

_____

_____

_____

_____

_____

2. How is the posture of your heart and mind?

_____

_____

_____

_____

_____

GO FORTH

Have I not commanded you?
Be strong and courageous.
–JOSHUA 1:9 (ESV)

G od gave *you* the vision, not them. Start the business. Write the book!

Whatever God told you to do, *start it today*! He will be with you as you do the things He has anointed your hand to do. For that to happen, you must take the first step. Your first step will represent many things—first stepping out on faith and becoming free. On this journey, you must follow what has been given to you.

This is a critical time when you will have to keep some things to yourself. In this season, every thought and idea cannot be shared, no matter how excited you are. You will have to operate in complete silence. You must *protect* that which the Lord is birthing through you. Oftentimes, we get excited and want to share what God has given us. That can be detrimental to your assignment. Let me expound.

There may be something you know God has instructed you to do and you share it with someone. If their response is not what you expect, at that very moment, they may have just talked you out of it or made you question what God has instructed you to do. In turn, it could cause you either to delay or, in some cases, abort what God has assigned you to do.

Secondly, we all want support. I get it. However, let's not get so caught up in looking for validation from people that we disregard the instruction and/or abort our purpose, especially for people who cannot see their own. God gave the assignment to you! They cannot see it and will not understand it. They are not *supposed* to see it or understand it. The vision was designed for you, *not them!*

It is my prayer that the tugging you feel in your spirit will give you the start you need to complete your assignment. Even if it does not make sense to you, know that you will understand at the appointed time. If it is a book, write whatever the Lord has instructed you to write. It doesn't matter if someone you know started it first. *Start today!* As you move forward in the assignment that God has set for you, remember that this isn't a race. Stay focused and consistent in your journey.

Heavenly Father, I pray that every assignment and project you have purposed your child to do will be done, without delay or need of validation from man.

I pray that you will be in the midst of every business deal, every meeting and every thought according to what you have ordained.

In Jesus' name. Amen.

 **Meditation Moments**

1. What has God told you to do that you keep delaying?

_____

_____

_____

_____

_____

2. Do you know that He didn't make a mistake when He placed the torch in your hand?

_____

_____

_____

_____

_____

3. How will you operate after the command: *Be strong and courageous?*

_____

_____

_____

_____

_____

WHAT'S ON YOUR MIND?

Let this mind be in you,
which was also in Christ Jesus.
–PHILIPPIANS 2:5 (NKJV)

The apostle Paul wrote Philippians to the church of Philippi. It has been called a love letter that rejuvenates the believer's spiritual life. We can gain many things from the letters of the apostle Paul: encouragement, warning, and instruction on daily living as believers.

To let something happen means we, the believers, must permit ourselves to change our minds! Our mind—our thoughts—is the controller which produces our actions. If we are not careful, our thoughts and behaviors will lead us to a place God never desired us to be.

By having the mind of Christ, we are led by wisdom, not our feelings. A mind of Christ allows the fruit of the Spirit to lead, not our flesh. When we don't allow ourselves to obtain the mind of Christ, negative thoughts turn into distractions, leading us to the space of fear, doubt and confusion. Detours are produced by delay of the purpose because of our words. Today, I pray that we make a sure choice to have the mind of Christ— not just for the time we set aside for prayer and consecration—but for the balance of our days! As a people of God, if we want to see something different, we must think differently. Proverbs 23:7 (KJV) says, *For as he thinketh in his heart, so is he*. Whatever you think becomes your reality. So, what's on your mind? If those things have been inconsistent with the thoughts of Christ, make a conscious choice to adopt the mind of Christ. Reshape and renew your thoughts. You will experience liberty that will change your actions and ultimately bring forth transformation.

Father, we lay our minds on the altar this day.
May you renew, transform, and align our thoughts
with yours. Help us to have the mind of Christ,
filled with wisdom and guided by the fruit of the Spirit.
As we surrender our thoughts to you,
lead us away from distractions and delays,
and lead us towards a path of purpose and clarity.

Father, cleanse me with hyssop, and I will be pure and whiter than snow. Today, I proclaim a fresh mindset and new thoughts. Thank you for freeing me and removing what no longer benefits me. I am grateful for your saving grace and mercy. Thank you for cleansing and eliminating what didn't serve a purpose.

In Jesus' name. Amen.

 *Meditation Moments*

1. What do you define as having the mind of Christ?

    _____

    _____

    _____

    _____

    _____

2. Have you invited God in to help you through the process of transfo‑ming your mind?

    _____

    _____

    _____

    _____

    _____

3. How will you embrace the journey of renewing your mind?

_____

_____

_____

_____

_____

STAY ON THE WALL

Pray without ceasing.
–1 THESSALONIANS 5:17 (KJV)

The Bible is full of instructions and commands. The directive in 1 Thessalonians 5:17 leads us to consistent communication with God—to pray not just once—but continually without ceasing. The primary purpose of prayer is to develop a relationship with God— intimate relationship and communion with our Heavenly Father. In the secret place is where we will receive revelation. In the secret place, you'll gain strength and wholeness. You will find peace in the secret place, even in the most unfavorable situation. In the secret place, you can be real and raw.

There is nothing God can't do as long as it's according to *His* will. There's no mountain that can't be moved. There is no disease that God can't heal. There is no heart that God can't mend, no bondage that God can't break, and no sin that God can't forgive. There is nothing the Father can't do. But will you take the time to pray? Can you take the time to enter His presence without distraction? Can you take the time to pray without a hidden agenda? Will you open your heart and pray to Him, laying down every weight and worry? Will you pray without ceasing?

Father, thank you for the ability to come to you in prayer for myself. Help me to keep you at the center of my entire day. May I be more disciplined and intentional with my communion with you. Father, help me to be steadfast in prayer and to be watchful with thanksgiving.

In Jesus' name. Amen.

 *Meditation Moments*

1. How often do you pray, meditate and seek God?

    _____

    _____

    _____

    _____

    _____

2. What is the posture of your heart when you go to God in prayer?

    _____

    _____

    _____

    _____

    _____

3. Do you believe wholeheartedly in the power of prayer?

_____

_____

_____

_____

_____

4. Are there specific times or places considered to be more conducive to prayer for you?

_____

_____

_____

_____

_____

PROMISE KEEPER

This is what the LORD says:
"When seventy years are completed for Babylon, I will
come to you and fulfill my good promise to bring you
back to this place. For I know the plans I have for you,"
declares the LORD, "plans to prosper you and not to
harm you, plans to give you hope and a future."
–JEREMIAH 29:10-11 (NIV)

---

*J*eremiah 29:11 in The Message Bible says it this way: *"I know what I'm doing. I have it all planned out— plans to take care of you, not abandon you, plans to give you the future you hope for."* God's response isn't necessarily an immediate escape from the difficult situation. He responds with this statement: "I have plans."

A plan defined by Merriam-Webster is, "A detailed formulation of a program of something."

God offers to us all a *plan, a detailed proposal*:

† A plan of reassurance

† A plan of security

† A plan of prosperity

Sometimes, before we fully see what God said, He will allow us to face some storms. He will allow us to face some valley seasons and some uncomfortable situations. But know this: If your stance remains firm, though your faith may waver, you don't lose sight of the plans God has for your life. In the midst of a storm, it is imperative that you hold on to your faith, not your feelings. If you are not careful, you won't see the manifestation of His glory because you've allowed your feelings/emotions to reside over temporary situations. In doing so, we then give the circumstance more power and control than God. That is why it is so critical to guard our hearts.

Proverbs 4:23 (NIV) says, *Above all else, guard your heart, for everything you do flows from it.* If we are not careful, what we perceive by way of experience will cause us to disrupt or demolish the plans God has assigned for us. If we do not control our feelings, the enemy uses feelings to manipulate and deceive. In seasons of *wait* vs. *weight*, we may view the season as an attack or punishment. Everything isn't the enemy. Sometimes God causes us to wait to build our faith or to mature us. The weight produces strength so that you can properly carry His promise. Many times, if God isn't moving as quickly as we think He should, it turns into, "God forgot about me."

As you are faithing your way through, you will be faced with trials and tribulations. John 16:33 (NKJV) says, *"These things I have spoken to you, that in Me you may have peace. In the world you will have tribulation; but be of good cheer, I have overcome the world."*

Though it may not feel good, God said that He would be with you always. He said that He would never leave you nor forsake you; don't allow what you feel to disrupt or kill the promise God made you.

Heavenly Father, I come needing help. Lord, help me to not allow my feelings to keep me from what you said. Even when the trial comes and I find myself caught up in my feelings versus your Word, Lord, please remind me that your plan is sure and true.

In Jesus' name. Amen.

Meditation Moments

1. Knowing that God's plan is sure and true, how will you respond to circumstances that arise the next time?

_____

_____

_____

_____

_____

2. How have you seen the effects of your feelings skewing your view of God and His Word concerning you?

_____

_____

_____

_____

_____

3. How have your experiences caused you to view God's promises as if they came from man?

_____

_____

_____

_____

_____

4. How do you perceive the promises of God? Do you believe they are conditional or unconditional, and how does this affect your faith?

_____

_____

_____

_____

_____

AUTHORITY OVER IT

For the weapons of our warfare are not carnal but mighty in God for pulling down strongholds, casting down arguments and every high thing that exalts itself against the knowledge of God, bringing every thought into captivity to the obedience of Christ.
–2 CORINTHIANS 10:4-5 (NKJV)

Do you understand who you are in God? Do you understand your power? Do you not know the authority you have in the spirit realm? *It* has already been placed on the inside of you! You already possess it! You have what it takes! *Now, it's time to walk in the authority.*

We serve notice to everything that attempts to exalt itself above the Word and knowledge of God. Listen up! The weapons we use in our battles are not physical, but they are mighty in God. They have the power to pull down strongholds, demolish arguments, and destroy everything that opposes the knowledge of God. We take every rebellious thought captive and make it obedient to Christ.

As someone who has authority over *it*, you possess the power to control anything that exalts itself above the Word of God. So, take charge and use your authority to ensure that *it* remains under your feet and does not become a threat to God's teachings. Spiritual matters call for spiritual tools. The Lord has already equipped you with the tools you need to carry you into victory. Ephesians 6 tells us what those tools are: the helmet of salvation, the shield of faith, the sword of the Spirit, the shoes of peace, the breastplate of righteousness and the belt of truth.

Father, I am standing, knocking and asking you to help my unbelief in areas where I waver. O Lord, I desire for my heart and mind to be filled with your Word. Help me grow in my knowledge of you. Help me to meditate on your Word, day and night, Lord. Your Word declared that I should study to show myself approved, the workman who needs not be ashamed, rightly dividing the Word of Truth. Your Word is the answer, and I will journey to grow deeper in it.

In Jesus' name. Amen.

Meditation Moments

1. Do you understand the importance of taking possession/authority over your thoughts?

_____

_____

_____

_____

_____

2. What ways will you *show up* as a partaker of authority over your life?

_____

_____

_____

_____

_____

3. Find the Scriptures below and say them aloud. Meditate on them.

But you belong to God, my dear children.
You have already won a victory over those people,
because the Spirit who lives in you is greater
than the spirit who lives in the world.
–JOHN 4:4 (NLT)

No weapon that is formed against you will prosper;
and every tongue that accuses you in judgement you
will condemn. This is the heritage of the servants of the
lor, and their vindication is from me, declares the lord.
–ISAIAH 54:17 (NIV)

No, in all these things we are more than
conquerors through him who loved us.
–ROMANS 8:37 (NIV)

But thanks be to God!
He gives us the victory through our Lord Jesus Christ.
–1 CORINTHIANS 15:57 (NIV)

I have given you authority to trample on
snakes and scorpions and to overcome all the
power of the enemy; nothing will harm you.
–LUKE 10:19

PURPOSE IN THE WAIT

But those who wait on the LORD shall renew their strength; they shall mount up with wings like eagles, they shall run and not be weary, they shall walk and not faint.
–ISAIAH 40:31 (NKJV)

*H*ave you ever been tired of waiting on God when it seems like God's moving too slow? Sometimes, it appears that He's not moving at all; so, you get into the mode of, "I'll take matters into my own hands." You haven't quite mastered the art of letting God handle it. You may have also been in the position that the longer you wait on the Lord, the heavier the weight gets! Though the weight may be heavy, the wait has purpose. God's waiting room is the most important space to encounter. It is where God tests our commitment and grows our faith. That's why you can't skip the waiting room, no matter how frustrating it may be.

Throughout Scripture, there were many individuals who found themselves in the waiting room. Abraham and Sarah waited many years for the fulfillment of God's promises of a son. Job endured much suffering and loss, but he continued to trust in God and waited for his restoration. As a result, his *weight*, and his *wait*, got him double. Hannah prayed fervently for a child and waited patiently for God to answer, and He did.

What are you doing while you wait? Are you weeping or are you worshipping? Are you living a consecrated life or living life frivolously? Are you praying or are you worrying? Are you meditating on Him, seeking the Father both day and night? In Isaiah 40:28, there were two questions: *Do you not know?* And, *Have you not heard?* Do you not know that God is eternal? Have you not heard that He is the Alpha and the Omega, the beginning and the end? Don't allow what you go through to cause you to dismiss what you already know about the God you believe.

Well, let's not stop there. How about the ways He's already made for you? The healing of sickness or disease. The deliverance He has already provided for you. Your position has to be in alignment with who you say God is to you. Submit to His power and authority. You can't be in control while waiting on God! His timing is perfect.

Father, I come to you asking for patience as I dwell in the waiting room. Father, I know that your timing is perfect; please help me relinquish control and know that all is working together for my good. I know that you are a man who cannot lie, and you will not withhold a good thing from me. Lord, as I wait, please help me to wait well.

In Jesus' name. Amen.

Meditation Moments

1. What area do you find yourself struggling with while you wait?

_____

_____

_____

_____

_____

2. In your waiting room process, has it been hard to relinquish control in totality?

_____

_____

_____

_____

_____

3. Waiting requires patience and requires you to trust. Can you trust God even though you don't currently see results?

_____

_____

_____

_____

_____

4. Can you identify any positive outcomes that have emerged from your waiting?

_____

_____

_____

_____

_____

PICK A SIDE

*But when you ask him, be sure that your faith
is in God alone. Do not waver, for a person
with divided loyalty is as unsettled as a wave
of the sea that is blown and tossed by the wind.*
–JAMES 1:6 (NLT)

Trusting and believing in God is a deeply personal decision, one that stems from individual experiences, upbringing, and personal reflections. For many, faith in God is a cornerstone of their lives, providing them with guidance, comfort, and a sense of purpose. Trusting in God, to them, means believing that there is a higher plan and purpose for their lives. Even if the path is not immediately clear, or if outcomes do not align with their prayers or expectations, they still believe.

When people pray and ask God for something, their faith often entails a belief that God will respond in the way that is best, though this may not always align with what they asked for. This perspective is rooted in the belief that God sees the bigger picture and knows what is ultimately beneficial for one's spiritual growth and life journey. It's about trusting in God's timing and wisdom, even when facing disappointment or when outcomes are different from what one hoped for.

On the other hand, there are individuals who may struggle with the concept of faith or trusting in a higher power. Their experiences, reasoning, or the challenges they face might lead them to question or not believe in the existence of God. This, too, is a valid perspective, as the journey of faith and belief is highly personal and can vary greatly from one person to another. Ultimately, whether or not one chooses to trust and believe in God, and to what extent they believe that God will fulfill their prayers, reflects their individual journey with faith. But there comes a time when you must choose "a side." Where are you going and what do you stand for? So often, we hang our hats on tomorrow. But what if you only have today?

Father, no more will I allow doubt to cloud my mind.
No more will I succumb to fear.

I stand firm in my beliefs, unwavering in my resolve. Father, guide my steps as I walk the path you have laid out for me. I embrace the strength within me, ready to face whatever challenges may come my way. With faith as my shield and determination as my sword, I march forward with confidence and purpose in you.
In Jesus' name. Amen.

 **Meditation Moments**

1. Do you struggle with trusting God?

   _____

   _____

   _____

   _____

   _____

2. Has there been a situation that caused a decrease in your faith?

   _____

   _____

   _____

   _____

   _____

3. As you move forward in your faith journey, how will you increase your faith?

_____

_____

_____

_____

4. Have you found any practices, such as prayer or meditation, helpful in connection or reconnecting with your faith?

_____

_____

_____

_____

5. Are there community groups or faith-based organizations that can support you in your journey?

_____

_____

_____

_____

GET IN ALIGNMENT

"Let us hold fast the confession of our hope without wavering, for He who promised is faithful."
-HEBREWS 10:23 (NKJV)

---

*A*ligning oreself with God's Word is a transformative practice that brings about spiritual alignment and personal breakthrough. God's Word is not merely a collection of ancient texts; it is a living, breathing guide that offers wisdom, direction, and promises for every aspect of life. When facing any situation, be it a challenge, a decision-making process, or a desire for personal growth, turning to what God has already declared about us and our circumstances is paramount This involves not only reading the Scriptures, but also embracing and believing in the truths they convey about God's love, plans, and promises for us.

To come into alignment with God's Word means to accept and affirm His declarations as the ultimate truth, above our feelings, circumstances, or worldly wisdom. It requires faith—a confident assurance in things unseen. By doing so, we align our thoughts, words, and actions with His will, making room for His power to work through us. This alignment is crucial for it opens the door to divine intervention and blessings. It is about making a conscious decision to fully trust in His plans (not your own), which are always for our good, even when they might not align with our immediate desires or understanding.

Filling your atmosphere with God's promises involves a deliberate effort to surround yourself with His Word. This can be through daily reading of the Bible, memorization of key verses that speak to your situation, or incorporating worship and praise music that echoes these truths. Speaking God's promises aloud, declaring them over your life, and sharing them with others not only reinforces your faith, but also serves as a powerful testimony of God's faithfulness. It's about creating an environment where God's Word is the foundation and authority, thereby allowing His peace, strength, and guidance to permeate every aspect of your life. In doing so, you open yourself to experiencing the fullness of God's blessings and purpose for you, grounded in the assurance that what He has promised, He will fulfill.

Lord, Your Word is alive and active, sharper than any two-edged sword, discerning the thoughts and intentions of the heart. Therefore, I immerse myself in Your Scriptures, allowing them to transform my thinking, renew my mind, and align my life with Your will. As I meditate on your promises, let them take root in my heart, producing faith and driving out doubt and fear. Your Word says that by your stripes, I am healed; I claim that healing over my body, mind, and spirit. You have promised to supply all my needs according to Your riches in glory. I trust in your provision and timing.

In Jesus' name. Amen.

 *Meditation Moments*

1. Coming into alignment means agreement. Are you ready to come into agreement with what and who God created you to be without reservation?

_____

_____

_____

_____

_____

2. What steps have you taken to ensure that you are in alignment with God?

_____

_____

_____

_____

_____

3. What area do you need assistance with?

_____

_____

_____

_____

_____

MELODIES OF FAITH

So then faith comes by hearing and hearing by the word of God.
-ROMANS 10:17 (NKJV)

In order to have faith in something or someone awareness of their existence is crucial.

"Faith comes by hearing." Right? What are you engaged in? What and to whom are you listening?

By actively engaging with the teachings of the gospel and opening their hearts to the grace and compassion of Jesus, individuals can cultivate a deep sense of connection and trust in something greater than themselves. Through the power of belief and understanding, one can find solace in moments of uncertainty and draw strength from the timeless wisdom found within the sacred Scriptures. As we continue to listen and learn, our faith grows stronger, anchoring us in a foundation of love and grace that transcends all earthly trials. So, let us keep our hearts attuned to the melodies of faith, and keep our spirits receptive to the divine symphony of hope that guides us on our journey toward everlasting peace and salvation.

Father, lead me to the right covering with the right biblical teaching that I need. I want more of you. Help me to know the Word for myself. I want to live according to your will and way. I do realize that it can only happen if I study to show myself approved. Illuminate my understanding and fill my heart with your Word.

In Jesus' name. Amen.

Meditation Moments

1. Since faith comes by hearing, what and to whom are you listening?

---

2. Who are you allowing to feed your spirit? Is it sound doctrine?

---

3. What you are being fed, and is it coming directly from Scripture?

_____

_____

_____

_____

_____

4. Do you study the Word of God for yourself?

_____

_____

_____

_____

_____

NEVER ALONE

*"But it is the spirit in a person, the breath of the
Almighty, that gives them understanding."*
–JOB 32:8 (NIV)

*"And the Spirit of the LORD will rest on Him—
The Spirit of wisdom and understanding, The Spirit of
counsel and strength, The Spirit of knowledge and of
the [reverential and obedient] fear of the LORD—"*
–ISAIAH 11:2 (AMP)

It is the Holy Spirit who gives the inspiration and understanding to what already exists in the spirit realm. Building on this understanding, it is essential to recognize the profound role that the Holy Spirit plays in the spiritual realm.

† The Holy Spirit serves as a guiding force, providing inspiration and clarity to individuals who seek spiritual enlightenment.

† Through the Holy Spirit, individuals can gain a deeper understanding of spiritual truths and principles that may be beyond human comprehension.

† The Holy Spirit acts as a bridge between the physical world and the spiritual realm, offering insights and revelations that can transform one's perspective on existence.

† Those who are attuned to the Holy Spirit are often able to tap into a higher plane of consciousness, allowing them to access divine wisdom and guidance.

† By cultivating a relationship with the Holy Spirit through prayer, meditation, and reflection, individuals can enhance their spiritual awareness and connection to the divine.

Will you be intentional and press into the presence of God? Tap into the advocate, the Holy Spirit, today. You depend on it! Yes, you. The Holy is available; the question is, "Are you available?" The Lord promised that He would not leave us. He said that He will give us another advocate to help us and be with us forever, which is the Spirit of truth.

Heavenly Father, I am grateful for your unwavering love and endless kindness that you shower upon me each day. Thank you for the Holy Spirit, whose gentle guidance and wisdom light my path and fill my heart with peace. I am truly blessed to have your presence in my life, guiding me through both the joys and challenges that come my way. Your love is a beacon of hope, and your kindness is a source of strength. Thank you for being my rock and my salvation. I submit to your will.

In Jesus' name. Amen.

Meditation Moments

1. Have you invited the Holy Spirit in?

_____

_____

_____

_____

_____

2. What teachings or Scriptures have helped you deepen your relationship with the Holy Spirit?

_____

_____

_____

_____

_____

3. How do you discern the voice of the Holy Spirit from your own thoughts and feelings?

_____

_____

_____

_____

_____

4. In what ways has the Holy Spirit influenced your decisions and actions?

_____

_____

_____

_____

_____

DRY BONES

This is what the Sovereign LORD says to these bones:
Look, I am about to infuse breath
into you and you will live.
-EZEKIEL 37:5 (NET)

*W*ill you speak life over what may seem to be the end or what has been pronounced dead? Nurture your faith. Let it be the guiding light that dispels any darkness or doubt. The sovereign Lord, the supreme ruler, has imparted the breath that will produce what you need to stand firm, to persevere through challenges, and to emerge victorious. Trust in His infinite wisdom and love, knowing that He is orchestrating every detail of your journey for your ultimate good, even at the brink of what seems to be death. Embrace the strength that comes from believing in His unwavering promises. Don't lose hope. Those dry bones will surely live. Let your heart be filled with courage and determination, knowing that the power of faith can bring life to what once seemed lifeless. As you walk through the valleys of despair, hold steadfast to the assurance that even the most barren places can bloom with new beginnings.

Father, I take you at your word. I know you can do all, except fail. I declare that these dry bones shall live. I thank you for your power and divine presence, for what appeared to be dead, you said, "Not so."
With unwavering faith, I trust in your promises and embrace the hope you have instilled within me. Every challenge, and every obstacle, is a steppingstone to greater glory. I am confident that your guidance will lead me through the darkest valleys into the light of triumph. As I stand in awe of your boundless grace, I am reminded that even in moments of doubt, your love remains steadfast and unyielding. So, with a heart full of gratitude, and a spirit fortified by your strength, I move forward, ready to witness the miraculous transformation you have in store. Let every breath be a testament to your unwavering faithfulness and every step a reflection of your divine will.

In Jesus' name. Amen.

Meditation Moments

1. Is there anything you desire the Lord to restore?

_____

_____

_____

_____

_____

2. Even if it appears to be lifeless, do you believe God can retore it if it's His will?

_____

_____

_____

_____

_____

3. Do you believe that you have the power to speak life
   into those situations and see them transformed by
   faith?

   _____

   _____

   _____

   _____

   _____

THE FINAL WORD

As you make your way through life on the journey of faith, there are numerous references that can help strengthen your faith. From sacred texts and teachings to personal experiences and moments of reflection, each step you take can be guided by the wisdom and inspiration found in these references. Remember to stay open to the signs and messages that come your way, for they may serve as reminders of the divine presence in your life. Embrace the journey with an open heart and a curious mind, and let these references be your companions along the path of faith.

Now faith is confidence in what we hope for and assurance about what we do not see.
–HEBREWS 11:1

I pray that out of his glorious riches he may strengthen you with power through his Spirit in your inner being, so that Christ may dwell in your hearts through faith. And I pray that you, being rooted and established in love.

–EPHESIANS 3:16-17

For we live by faith, not by sight.

–2 CORINTHIANS 5:7

And without faith it is impossible to please God, because anyone who comes to him must believe that he exists and that he rewards those who earnestly seek him.

–HEBREWS 11:6

Then Jesus said, "Did I not tell you that if you believe, you will see the glory of God?"

–JOHN 11:40

Consider it pure joy, my brothers and sisters, whenever you face trials of many kinds, because you know that the testing of your faith produces perseverance.

–JAMES 1:2-3

Though you have not seen him, you love him; and even though you do not see him now, you believe in him and are filled with an inexpressible and glorious joy, for you are receiving the end result of your faith, the salvation of your souls.

–1 PETER 1:8-9

"'If you can'?" said Jesus.
"Everything is possible for one who believes."
– MARK 9:23

Jesus said to her, "I am the resurrection and the life.
The one who believes in me will live, even though they
die; and whoever lives by believing in me will never die.
Do you believe this?"
–JOHN 11:25-26

Accept the one whose faith is weak,
without quarreling over disputable matters.
–ROMANS 14:1

if you believe, you will receive
whatever you ask for in prayer.
–MATTHEW 21:22

"Go," said Jesus, "your faith has healed you."
Immediately he received his sight and
followed Jesus along the road.
–MARK 10:52

Then Jesus declared, "I am the bread of life. Whoever
comes to me will never go hungry, and whoever
believes in me will never be thirsty.
–JOHN 6:35

*For in the gospel the righteousness of God is revealed—
a righteousness that is by faith from first to last, just as
it is written: "The righteous will live by faith."*
–ROMANS 1:17

*So in Christ Jesus you are all children of God through
faith, for all of you who were baptized into Christ have
clothed yourselves with Christ.*
–GALATIANS 3:26-27

*For God so loved the world, that he gave his
one and only Son, that whoever believes
in him shall not perish but have eternal life.*
–JOHN 3:16

*Is anyone among you sick? Let them call the elders of
the church to pray over them and anoint them with oil
in the name of the Lord. And the prayer offered in faith
will make the sick person well; the Lord will raise them
up. If they have sinned, they will be forgiven.*
–JAMES 5:14-15

*He replied, "Because you have so little faith. Truly I tell
you, if you have faith as small as a mustard seed, you
can say to this mountain, 'Move from here to there,'
and it will move. Nothing will be impossible for you."*
–MATTHEW 17:20

Jesus answered, "The work of God is this: to believe in the one he has sent."
–JOHN 6:29

Whoever believes in me, as Scripture has said, rivers of living water will flow from within them.
–JOHN 7:38

As Scripture says, "Anyone who believes in him will never be put to shame."
–ROMANS 10:11

Then Jesus told him. "Because you have seen me, you have believed; blessed are those who have not seen and yet have believed."
–JOHN 20:29

Hearing this, Jesus said to Jairus, "Don't be afraid; just believe, and she will be healed."
–LUKE 8:50

Who is it that overcomes the world? Only the one who believes that Jesus is the Son of God.
–1 JOHN 5:5

Therefore, since we have been justified through faith, we have peace with God through our Lord Jesus Christ.
–ROMANS 5:1

I tell you, you can pray for anything, and if you believe that you've received it, it will be yours.

−MARK 11:24 (NLT)

But when you ask him, be sure that your faith is in God alone. Do not waver, for a person with divided loyalty is as unsettled as a wave of the sea that is blown and tossed by the wind.

−JAMES 1:6 (NLT)

Don't worry about anything; instead, pray about everything. Tell God what you need and thank him for all he has done. Then you will experience God's peace, which exceeds anything we can understand. His peace will guard your hearts and minds as you live in Christ Jesus.

−PHILIPPIANS 4:6-7 (NLT)

Trust in the LORD with all your heart and lean not on your own understanding in all your ways submit to him, and he will make your paths straight.

−PROVERBS 3:5-6

A MESSAGE FROM THE AUTHOR

A beacon of hope guides you through the darkest of times. It is a source of strength that empowers you to face any challenge with courage. Remember, you are never alone on this journey. Grace and faith walk beside you, lighting the path ahead. Let your heart be filled with love, your mind with wisdom, and your spirit with peace as you embrace the gift of salvation. May it be a constant source of comfort and joy, reminding you of the boundless grace that surrounds you always. Stay steadfast, stay true, and may your faith continue to flourish in the light of divine love.

As you journey through this life of faith, I declare that the old life is gone, and all shall be made new according to God's will, plan, and purpose, in Jesus' name. As you embark on this journey, remember that God has already gone before you. There is a divine plan and purpose for your life. May the power of His glory overshadow you on every side. I pray that the Father's unfailing, unwavering, unconditional love is a direct, consistent reminder of who you are and whose you are. The foundation and bricks have been laid with every step calculated with you in mind. With each step, remember these words:

"The Lord himself goes before you and will be with you; he will never leave you nor forsake you. Do not be afraid; do not be discouraged."
–DEUTERONOMY 31:8 (NIV)

May God continue to keep you is my consistent prayer.

Blessings,

Cecilia N. Hubbard

ABOUT THE AUTHOR

*W*hile many people are chasing accolades and awards, she's on a mission to simply fulfill the purpose of God in her life—and help others do the same. For minister, author and speaker, Cecilia N. Hubbard, life has been far from easy. However, even in the midst of her trials, tribulations and troubles, she understands wholeheartedly that she is both called and chosen to support, motivate and empower others through every unique transition and journey. A beacon of hope, love and light to many, she knows firsthand that although each one's journey may be different, by standing firm and having faith in God, nothing will be impossible. In 2018, the "Standing on Faith" movement was born. For Cecilia, faith became her lifestyle, not just a movement.

Licensed as a minister of the Gospel in 2023, Cecilia seeks to not only help others strengthen their relationship with God—but to find their authentic purpose and walk in freedom and fulfillment. In addition to being the CEO of One Unique Vision Events since 2010, she holds an associate degree from The University of Phoenix and founded the Cecilia Nicole Collection in 2022. Whereas many people are simply looking to make a deposit into the lives of others, Cecilia seeks to transform hearts and minds—whether she is speaking, preaching or writing. She is also actively pursuing her bachelor's degree in business.

An intercessor with a deep passion and heart for prayer, Cecilia leads the Faithing Your Way through Prayer Call to help others strengthen their faith and connection with God through prayer. Committed to serving in this capacity with humility, compassion and unwavering faith, she considers her work as an intercessor to be one of the most fulfilling and meaningful aspects of her life. In her debut book, *The Journey: Faithing Your Way Through*, she takes readers on an authentic journey of self-discovery, faith exploration and strengthening in their relationship with the Father. Recognizing that faith is deeply personal and ever evolving, Cecilia empowers readers to navigate real-life situations as they find peace and purpose on their continual spiritual journey.

For booking or speaking engagements,
email Cecilianicoleministries@gmail.com or visit
www.Cecilianicoleministries.com.